How to Write Effective Teaching Notes & Teach Case Studies Effectively?

Dr. Kisholoy Roy

© **Kisholoy Roy**

First Edition

Copyright of this book solely rests with the author and no part of this book shall be reproduced or transmitted in any form across any medium without the consent of the author

If our lives are a Case Study then our parents are our Teaching Notes!!

Preface

In the year 2015, I authored *How to Write and Teach Case Studies Effectively?* and then in 2017, I authored *Do Case Studies have a Shelf Life?* (also to be found online as *How to Enhance Shelf Life of Case Studies?*). In both these books, the primary focus has been on writing case studies effectively.

Case Studies have become a significant tool of learning in management education since case based teaching has been continuously evolving and proliferating across institutes in India and abroad. This form of teaching was first introduced at Harvard Business School way back in the 1920s. Writing an effective case thus is extremely critical which I have detailed in my previous books. My second book went a step further in detailing how a case writer and a host of other entities can ensure the longevity of a case study. There are certain ingredients and approach that go into the making of a durable case which were adequately mentioned in my second book. I did mention about some basics of teaching case studies at B-schools in my book *How to…Effectively?*

This book titled *How to Write Effective Teaching Notes & Teach Case Studies Effectively?* can well be considered to complete my authored trilogy on management case studies. This book not just goes a step further or rather couple of steps further into the exact and effective approach to teaching cases but it also details about writing effective teaching notes. Teaching notes go a long way in making teachers understand the efficacy of a case study and its suitability of usage in the context of a particular curriculum. It also offers teachers guidance/suggestion as how to conduct a class on case based teaching.

Over here, I will like to take this opportunity to thank *The Case Centre* team based in the UK (htttps://www.thecasecentre.org) for them have always been the pioneers to introduce newer models and theories to case teaching and learning. Case teaching methodology is something that always needs to stay contemporary in order to keep appealing to target audiences and keeping the interest alive about learning through case studies and that is exactly what this organization has been doing for several decades now. One of the largest repositories on case studies and teaching notes in the world, *The Case Centre* is certainly an avenue that inspires many educators like me to remain an ever alert student to newer developments happening in the field of case and teaching note writing and case teaching.

Any case based teaching will b considered effective only when a teacher actively observes moderates and evaluates participants in the discussion. He is ideally to don the role of a facilitator and not merely stay an authoritative teacher/passive observer. This allows minds of pupils to open up, think laterally and enjoy the activity of devising multiple solutions to various issues and problems raised in a case study.

As an author, I hope that both the research and teaching community will find this effort worthy of being read, imbibed and applied.

Happy Learning!!

Dr Kisholoy Roy
August, 2018

PART A:

WRITING EFFECTIVE TEACHING NOTES

Preamble to PART A

There was a point of time when case studies based on various subjects and issues were developed and the same were later adopted by teachers and administered in classes. There were two major drawbacks of this phenomenon. First of all, it often so happened that a case writer collated the data available from various published sources or constructed the case based on certain empirical studies or activities without giving much thought to the learning objectives of the case study. To the case writer, it was purely about his or her creative pursuit and a way to express one's expertise in a subject area as a writer. Secondly, the professors often took a case for administering in class based on some preliminary study and understanding and not with an extremely informed idea about the case and the learning outcomes from it. This in turn led to diminished learning and students hardly derived any significance of learning through a case.

However times have changed and therefore we find that case repositories like The Case Centre (www.thecasecentre.org) are hardly offering solitary case studies now a days on their platform. The organization is offering something called *'Case Packs'*. These case packs comprise of a *Case Abstract, Case Study* and *Teaching Note* to the case study. It is being increasingly observed that professors at various leading B-schools are absolutely inclined to having teaching notes to case studies before they administer a case in a class of students. They are interested to be better informed about a case study and the learning outcomes from it before administering the same in class. Teaching notes help faculties understand the suitability of a case for a particular class and subject and thus this enables students to better experience the learning that happens through a case study.

In this book, before I introduce teaching notes in a more detailed manner and ways to develop an effective teaching note, I have included two case studies of different formats and flavors for the readers to study them first and then understand how the corresponding teaching notes have been developed.

The first case study is a variant of a case study called *Case Flyer*. Just like there is a difference between case studies and *Caselets* in terms of length and treatment, there is a difference existing between case studies and case flyers. Case flyers are classroom discussion boards developed from published articles. Often the class may be given a solitary article or may be given an article compiled from two different published sources and then we find a series of questions after that which is supposed to trigger classroom discussions. Unlike a case study, a case flyer is not about a writer presenting a technical issue in his own words but just includes sentences and paragraphs as they have been published in original with due acknowledgement prominently displayed within the case flyer. The case flyer mentioned in this book is based on the premise of celebrity endorsements. The second is a case study on Xiaomi and its emphatic performance in India over the last few years.

The author suggests his readers to go through the case flyer and the case study first and then proceed to the corresponding teaching notes after understanding the ingredients and structure of an effective teaching note that have been mentioned in the section *About Teaching Notes*. Readers will also find that there are few differences in the way a teaching note to a case flyer and a teaching note to a case study are structured.

CASE FLYER

Celebrity Endorsements and Brands: Made for Each Other?

Expected Learning Outcomes

- Debating the need for celebrity endorsements to be adopted by marketers/advertisers
- Analyzing the dual effect of celebrities on brands
- Brainstorming ways of enhancing effectiveness of celebrity endorsements

Celebrity endorsements can be a double-edged sword and Snapdeal got the taste of it when thousands of users deleted its app and threatened to disassociate themselves from the brand that Aamir Khan endorses.

Snapdeal on Wednesday sought to distance itself from Aamir Khan's remarks by saying the comments were made by the actor in his personal capacity. At the same time, other top brands of India Inc such as Titan, Samsung, Coke, Emami, Tata Sky and Godrej found themselves being dragged into the controversy for their erstwhile association with him. On social media, many users were seen running campaigns to encourage others to boycott brands and services that Khan had endorsed in the past. "After #BootOutSnapdeal it's turn of @samsung @TataSky @CocaCola & Titan. Either remove @aamir_khan or face boycott," said a tweet from Puneet Sharma. Apart from Snapdeal, none of the brands mentioned above are currently using Khan as brand ambassador.

Similarly, after drawing flak on social media and watching its app being downgraded on Google Play Store by Khan's detractors, Snapdeal moved into damage control mode. The Gurgaon-based etailer said: "Snapdeal is neither connected nor plays a role in comments made by Aamir Khan in his personal capacity. Snapdeal is a proud Indian company built by passionate young Indians focused on building an inclusive digital India. Every day, we are positively impacting thousands of small businesses and millions of consumers in India. We

This is a flawed logic. Brands don't buy into brand ambassadors' personal opinions. @snapdeal shouldn't face this

SACHIN BANSAL | CEO, FLIPKART

will continue towards our mission of creating one million successful online entrepreneurs in India."

Sachin Bansal of Flipkart came out in defence of its e-commerce rival. "This is a flawed logic. Brands don't buy into brand ambassadors personal opinions. @snapdeal shouldn't face this," Bansal tweeted.

While celebrities, a favourite marketing conduit for products, could land a brand in trouble with a stray comment or behavior, these incidents are ephemeral, make little difference to consumer preferences and cannot destroy a brand's selling point unless the endorser is criminally indicted, feel most brand experts. "I think these incidents are more of a storm in a tea cup. Public memory is short and these blips get forgotten and forgiven in a few days. It's only when their action is irrevocable that a brand would let go of its ambassador, like it happened with Lance Armstrong. In India, most cases are temporary and I can't think of any actor or sports star who was blacklisted to a point of not being saleable," says Sumanto Chattopadhyay, executive creative director, South Asia, Ogilvy. His case in point: Salman Khan, once the bad boy of the industry who now belongs to the most expensive and illustrious league of endorsers in the country.

Ad filmmaker Pradeep Sarkar argues that "public and corporates understand whatever is going on with regards to Mr Khan's comments is silly and does not make sense. In terms of brands thinking twice before getting a celebrity on board, I don't think events like this would affect that. At the end of the day, the celebrity endorsing a brand has responsibility with the campaign and not what he or she says in personal capacity." While most believe that consumers will eventually buy a brand that benefits them, the little collateral damage that it can bring to the brand is driven by the fact that the pre-hire contract is not watertight in the country when it comes to signing up a celebrity nor are the celebrities briefed on do's and don'ts in public, which often leads both the endorser and endorsee into troubled waters.

> I think public and corporates understand whatever is going on with regards to Mr (Aamir) Khan's comments is silly and does not make sense ...At the end of the day, the celebrity endorsing a brand has responsibility with the campaign and not what he or she says in personal capacity
>
> **PRADEEP SARKAR** | AD FILMMAKER

"With polarized opinions, a brand does benefit from it but that said there is a silent background check done on a celeb and if he happens to be a secret alcoholic, druggie or woman beater, one would keep out of endorsements," said ad-guru Prahlad Kakkar.

Suhel Seth, a brand and marketing consultant for some of the country's top business houses, has opposed the idea of celebrity endorsement for years. His reason being "Brands carry a huge risk when they do so. Celebrity pre-hire contracts and processes aren't watertight in our country and the clauses are limited to money, appearances and conflicting categories. With social media on troll mode, celebrities often lead themselves to being exposed and result in a discussion, unnecessary for the brand," he says.

Arun Pandey of Rhiti Sports, which manages some high-profile celebrities' endorsements deals with corporates, believes otherwise. "This will not affect celebrity endorsements and the rapport with a corporate. Every celebrity signs a deal with a company for professional reasons and fulfills the need of the campaign but neither parties have got anything to do with personal comments of popular faces who endorse various brands."

BRAND BACKLASH

WHILE BRANDS RIDE ON THE POPULARITY OF CELEBRITIES, THEY ALSO FEEL THE HEAT WHEN THE STARS THAT ENDORSE THEM LAND IN CONTROVERSIES. HERE ARE A FEW EXAMPLES...

SALMAN KHAN Thums Up dropped the actor in 2001-02 after he was accused of killing a blackbuck and drink driving, which left one dead & 4 injured

TIGER WOODS Global brands like Gatorade, GM, Accenture and AT&T dropped the golf star in 2010-11 after his extramarital affairs became public

KOBE BRYANT Sprite, McDonald's and Nutella didn't renew contracts after the NBA superstar was accused of rape in 2004

LANCE ARMSTRONG Nike, AB InBev, Trek Bicycle, FRS and Honey Stinger, among others, terminated contracts with the cyclist in 2012 after he admitted to doping. Till then hailed as the greatest athlete of all time, Armstrong was also stripped off his 7 Tour de France titles

MICHAEL PHELPS Kellogg ended contract with the Olympic gold medallist swimmer after photos of him smoking pot appeared

KATE MOSS: H&M dropped ad campaign featuring the supermodel in 2005 after a London tabloid carried photos of her smoking cocaine. Burberry followed suit, Chanel did not renew contract with her

SANJAY DUTT Kolkata-based Rupa & Co stopped airing ads featuring Dutt after he was convicted under the Arms Act in 2007 in connection with the 1993 Mumbai blasts

MIKE TYSON He lost millions in endorsement money from Pepsi after his wife accused him of abuse. Other sponsors too followed suit in 1988

WAYNE ROONEY Coca-Cola did not renew its contract with the Manchester United striker after reports in 2010 accused him of cheating on his pregnant wife with prostitutes

CHRIS BROWN The hip-hop singer was dropped from 'Got Milk' campaign and Wrigley pulled off ads featuring him in 2009 after he was accused of assaulting ex-girlfriend Rihanna

AMITABH BACHCHAN His decision to shun IIFA in Sri Lanka amid protests by Tamil film industry saw the actor being removed as the brand ambassador of the award show after 10 years

MADONNA Pepsi put its popular commercial featuring Madonna on hold in 1989 after the pop star's 'Like A Prayer' video enraged the Catholics and the Vatican released a statement banning her from appearing in

JUSTIN GATLIN Nike suspended contract with Gatlin after he tested positive for testosterone and was stripped off his 100m gold in 2004 Athens Olympics

OSCAR PISTORIUS Oakley cancelled its contract with Pistorius and Nike didn't renew its in 2013 after the blade runner was charged with the murder of his girlfriend

O J SIMPSON The former American football star was the face of Hertz rental cars, which reportedly paid him $500,000 a year. The company, however, dropped him when allegations of domestic abuse surfaced in 1992. Simpson later became infamous for allegedly murdering his ex-wife Nicole Brown & her friend

STEPHANIE RICE Australian Olympic gold medallist swimmer was dropped by Jaguar in 2010 after her anti-gay tweets following Australia's rugby win on South Africa. Jaguar also took back

---

This Case Flyer has been compiled from the following published sources:

- *http://timesofindia.indiatimes.com/tech/tech-news/Aamirs-remarks-his-own-says-Snapdeal-heat-on-more-brands/articleshow/49928547.cms*
- *http://timesofindia.indiatimes.com/business/india-business/Its-a-storm-in-a-tea-cup-Brand-experts/articleshow/49928587.cms*

Assignment Questions

Celebrity Endorsements: To Be or Not To Be

1. 'Celebrity endorsements are no different than other form of advertising as because it is driven by an idea and if the idea works well with the target audience, the endorsements will work too else it is doomed to fail.' Do you agree? Enumerate your thoughts.
2. 'Not all product categories require a celebrity.' Present your view point on this statement.
3. Opposing the idea of celebrity endorsements, Suhel Seth opined, "Brands carry a huge risk when they do so. Celebrity pre-hire contracts and processes aren't watertight in our country and the clauses are limited to money, appearances and conflicting categories. With social media on troll mode, celebrities often lead themselves to being exposed and result in a discussion, unnecessary for the brand." Make a critical appreciation of Seth's statement.

Celebrity Endorsement: A Double-edged Sword

1. The negative effects of celebrity endorsements are ephemeral while its positive effects are long term in nature. Cite your observations in favor of or against this statement.
2. "This is a flawed logic. Brands don't buy into brand ambassadors' personal opinions. @snapdeal shouldn't face this," Do you agree with Bansal's

statement? Present your observations with suitable reasoning.
3. '..thousands of users deleted its app and threatened to disassociate themselves from the brand that Aamir Khan endorses.' As a consumer of brands around you, do you subscribe to such consumer actions? Present your thoughts in detail.

Celebrity Endorsements: Ways of Enhancing their Effectiveness

1. "With so much riding on the image of a celebrity and companies willing to devote a large chunk of their budget to ensure that a famous face brings visibility to the brand and boosts sales, most marketeers in their rush to sign up a celebrity, fail to tap into the different ways in which a celebrity's persona could colour the brand."[1] How do you propose to amend this flawed approach of marketers?
2. Should restrictions be imposed on celebrities in the celebrity contract as far as saying or doing things in one's 'personal capacity' is concerned? Present your view point through appropriate reasoning.
3. Suggest certain aspects to be incorporated in the pre-hire contracts signed with celebrities to make such documents more 'watertight'?

---

[1] *http://timesofindia.indiatimes.com/business/india-usiness/Its-a-storm-in-a-tea-cup-Brand-xperts/articleshow/49928587.cms*

CASE STUDY

Xiaomi in India: The Rise of the Chinese Challenger in Indian Smartphone Market

Abstract

This case study details the rise of Xiaomi in the Indian smartphone market. There were certain distinct lacunae existing in the market before Xiaomi started its operations in the year 2014 in India. The company successfully tackled the initial operational hurdles and wooed the Indian customers with smartphones that well defined the idea of value proposition. Sustained constructive efforts in the Indian markets allowed the company to surpass Samsung as the leader in the smartphone category in India.

Pedagogical Objectives

- To analyze and comprehend the nature of Indian smartphone market
- To examine the market entry strategies adopted by Xiaomi to make its initial presence felt in India
- To analyze the factors that have contributed to the success of Xiaomi in Indian smartphone market

Xiaomi in India: The Rise of the Chinese Challenger in Indian Smartphone Market

"I believe our constant innovation across our products, operating model and our commitment to India has helped us win over our MI fans."

- Manu Jain (Vice President, Xiaomi India)

Indian smartphone market has always been a play field of Nokia, Apple and Samsung where smartphones meant a premium to pay. Manufacturers like Micromax, Lava etc. were making phones but they never gave that ease and freedom to the consumers. Xiaomi entered India in 2014. The first phone MI3 was a mid-range phone but then a significant event happened when Xiaomi started selling budget series phone Redmi 1s. The manufacturer created a niche for its smartphone brand by executing flash sales on online shopping sites like Flipkart, which resulted in stock outs within matter of minutes. Hugo Barra former VP of Xiaomi India was more focused on the budget range as he felt that the Indian smartphone market was a price sensitive market. It was really incredible to find the brand rising to the top of the charts toppling its established competitors like Samsung without any celebrity endorsements or intensive marketing efforts. Value based pricing was one of the major reasons for the success of Xiaomi in India. This strategy helped build a community around the brand. Innovative and high performance phones and accessories have enabled Xiaomi develop an interesting and saleable product portfolio over the years.

A Humble Beginning

2014 was the year when Xiaomi India held an event to launch their first phone MI3 in India, Hugo Barra launched the phone at a staggering and ground breaking price of ₹13,999 when the phones with same specifications were no way near the price

Exhibit - I: Price Comparison of MI3 and LG Nexus 5

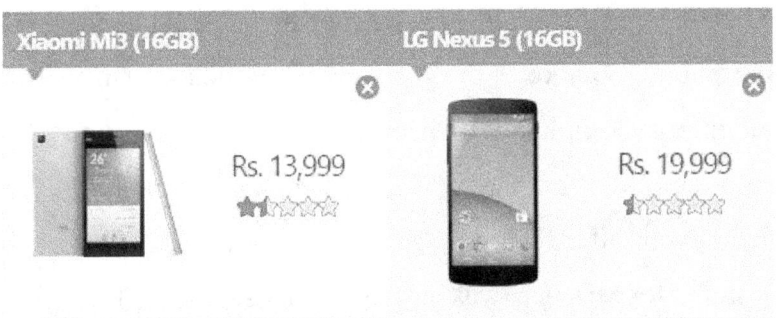

Source:https://www.smartprix.com/mobiles/xiaomi_mi3_16gb vs_lg_nexus_5_16gb_-c1101ly018t6_11013nuueyb.php

Xiaomi has always been the company that has priced their products closest to their bill of material without compromising the component quality and performance compared to other premium smartphones. That has been the key to their success. Xiaomi cashed on people's new found interest in buying electronic gadgets online and thus they effectively placed their first product on Flipkart. After the success of Redmi 1s the company looked to go for the release of different and advanced models of smartphone from its stable like MI3 and MI4. The phone did not hit the Indian shores like the previous ones. Then the company came with more pocket friendly Redmi 2 which was also value for money device. Xiaomi soon started getting better vibes from the market.

Hurdles on the way

Even after becoming the new cynosure of the Indian smartphone market the company faced many challenges. Complaints of heating issues were on the rise as the Mi4 hit the market. Sales were tumbling down even after being a mid-range device as the consumer experience was not quite satisfactory. The most controversial device of Xiaomi India was the Redmi Note 3G as people were accusing the company for data theft and sending the data to the Chinese servers (**Exhibit-II**).

Not only this but the Redmi Note 3G was also found to get into turmoil because of patent infringement with Ericson. Another challenge was in the area of establishing greater number of service centers as the existing number was not quite wholesome from customer service viewpoint plus competitors like ASUS were also making their presence felt in the increasingly saturated Indian smartphone market.

Exhibit-II: Gaqdgets360 reports Data Theft

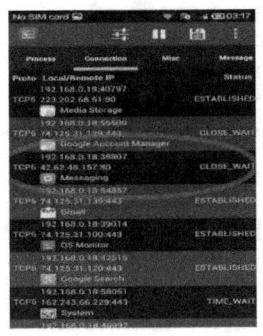

OCWorkbench, citing a Taiwanese publication, suggested that the budget Xiaomi Redmi Note, which was announced for the Indian market alongside the Mi 3 (Review | Pictures), was secretly sending data to a China-based server.

In addition, [the OCWorkbench report notes] a Hong Kong-based IMA Mobile user Kenny Li claims to have tested the Redmi Note smartphone, and found it was automatically connecting to an IP address hosted in China and sending data back when connected to a Wi-Fi network. Li also claimed that the Xiaomi Redmi Note was sending information to the Chinese server at a much lower data transmission rate when connected to a 3G network.

Interestingly, the Redmi Note was reportedly found transmitting data in the background even after being rooted or after being flashed with another firmware on top. OCWorkbench speculates that the transmission process had been hardcoded into the Xiaomi Redmi Note. The site noted that the company's cloud service called MiCloud was switched off during the testing.

Source: https://gadgets.ndtv.com/mobiles/news/is-xiaomi-secretly-sending-smartphone-user-data-to-chinese-servers-567686

Complaints regarding poor after sales service and the company's inability to meet the rising demand of consumers for Xiaomi smartphones were some of the other major issues The later contributed to reports of black marketing of Miphones.

Journey to the top

As on date, the company has been there in Indian market for quite sometime. The company has been expanding its dealer network across the country and is also in the process of launching new exclusive stores to showcase its range of products.

Xiaomi has been selling its smartphones both in the online as well as in the offline space and it has been observed that the major part of the smartphone buying is happening in the offline space. The company has been targeting the selfie obsessed audiences in both online and offline channels with its select products. Xiaomi not only tied up with stores where they can sell products offline but also they set-up MI HOME (exclusive Xiaomi outlets across India), similar to the execution of Apple stores where people can experience the products and buy them. The sale reports reflected the growth in the market share of the company after the nationwide set-up of the MI HOMEs. In 2018, the company ranks 2nd in terms of market share in the Indian smartphone market (**Exhibit-III**).

Exhibit-III: The IDC quarterly report of Q2 in 2017

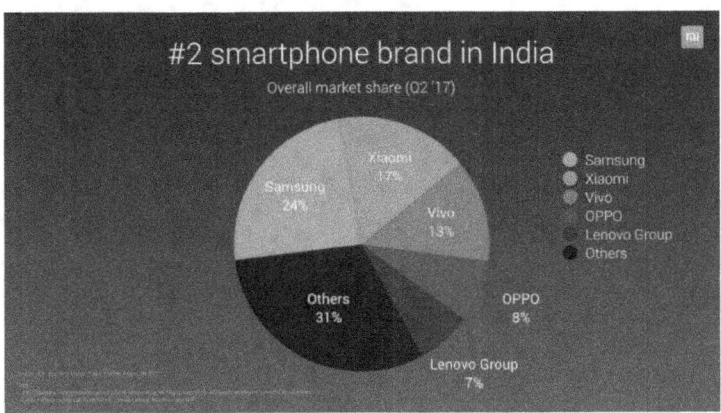

Xiaomi was forecasted to surpass Samsung after the year 2017 but the company managed to achieve that feat by the end of Q4 of 2017; the credit for which should go to the success of Redmi Note 4 as it was the most sold smartphone of the year 2017 (**Exhibit-IV**).

Credit not only goes to the product but also to the community the company has been building around its products. MI Forums, MI Community have significant role to play in the success of the company. The community members known as MI Fans have always been given sufficient regard and recognition by Xiaomi which has made consumer bonding with the company stronger over time.

Exhibit-IV: The IDC quarterly report Q4 2017

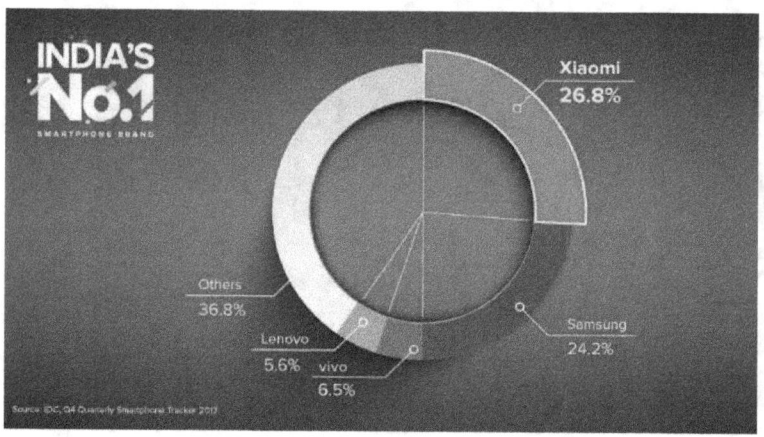

The trend of replacing smartphones on frequent basis has been on the rise mostly among the youth in this country and Xiaomi has cashed on this opportunity by launching more budget friendly quality devices. The value based pricing of Xiaomi made sure that competitors like Micromax's YU brand fail to keep the Chinese handset maker concerned for long. One of the contributors for the low pricing of Xiaomi is the 'Make in India' initiative taken by Xiaomi, opening two manufacturing facilities in India[11]. This has saved import duty and helped in developing customer-friendly pricing for their products giving them an edge over competition. Xiaomi have also treaded the path of future proofing their phones with narrowing down their displays of the phone which started with MI MIX line up. MI MIX line-up said to be the concept phone for the consumers as it reflected their futuristic design of no-edge displays.

The Road Ahead

Xiaomi, as per industry reports is the market leader in the Indian smartphone territory which leads to the question of how cans the company maintain its lead over competition? The company is presently more focused on bringing their ecosystem products like MI Band, MI TV and MI Bag pack etc. to the Indian market. MI has always focused on the innovation and bringing the products at best prices possible. The company might look to cement their place at the top but there are established competitors like Samsung, ASUS. The moves that Xiaomi make need to be differentiated and as per market requirements so that they keep striking the right chord with customers.

References

https://economictimes.indiatimes.com/opinion/interviews/xiaomi-to-cross-2-bn-revenue-this-year-may-consider-exports-manu-jain-xiaomi-india-vp/articleshow/60392432.cms

http://c.mi.com/thread-109563-1-1.html

http://www.bgr.in/news/xiaomi-after-sales-service-in-india-a-closer-look-at-the-companys-efforts-towards-customer-satisfaction/

http://www.bgr.in/news/you-wont-be-able-to-buy-a-xiaomi-redmi-note-5-pro-with-cash-on-delivery-anymore/

http://www.business-standard.com/article/companies/xiaomi-launches-redmi-y-series-selfie-smartphones-ropes-in-katrina-kaif-117110200718_1.html

http://www.business-standard.com/article/companies/xiaomi-launches-redmi-y-series-selfie-smartphones-ropes-in-katrina-kaif-117110200718_1.html

http://www.mi.com/in/service/mihome/

https://gadgets.ndtv.com/mobiles/news/xiaomi-redmi-note-4-most-selling-smartphone-cy-2017-counterpoint-1804587

https://economictimes.indiatimes.com/opinion/interviews/xiaomi-to-cross-2-bn-revenue-this-year-may-consider-exports-manu-jain-xiaomi-india-vp/articleshow/60392432.cms

http://www.fonearena.com/blog/140594/yu-vs-mi-reminds-us-why-competition-and-choice-are-great.html

http://indianexpress.com/article/technology/tech-news-technology/xiaomi-redmi-4a-now-has-a-second-factory-in-india-manufactures-one-phone-a-second-4577623/

Assignment Questions

1. What are the various marketing strategies to be used by an international marketer in its global expansion efforts?

2. Comment on the market entry strategies adopted by Xiaomi for the Indian market?

3. What were the major stumbling blocks that Xiaomi initially experienced in India?

4. How did Xiaomi go about addressing the 'availability quotient' of its smartphones in India?

5. What have been the various factors that have contributed to Xiaomi's success in India?

6. What are the aspects that have worked in favor of Xiaomi and the potential challenges it faces in India?

About Teaching Notes

In any case based learning scenario, it is the teacher who selects a case study for the class. He is the entity who decides which case study will best facilitate students' understanding of a subject. He is the person who estimates which case study will trigger suitable discussions, debates and enhanced learning. But then how can a professor conclude the 'fit' of a case study for a class? There has to be something which will facilitate this conclusion and that is a teaching note. It is the teaching note that enables a professor to arrive at a suitable understanding of the contents of a case and the learning outcomes that can be expected out of it. When it comes to selling of cases from case repositories like *The Case Centre*, case studies accompanied by teaching notes sell faster than those which are without any teaching notes. The pedagogical objectives of a case study are better emphasized through a teaching note.

A teaching note is supposed to be an instruction manual of teaching a case that it accompanies, and therefore it needs to meet the likely needs of the faculty who intends to use case studies in his classes. The quality of the teaching note depends on how well it offers meaningful step-by-step guidance for instructors, without any additional research. The objective of a teaching note is to highlight that how are professors to deal with the information contained in the case, how to analyze it and use it in the classroom discussion in order to achieve the learning goals.

A teaching note is a guide to both instructors who are in the process of deciding whether to teach a case and to those who have decided to teach a case. It highlights the teaching objectives of a case as well as the academic value an instructor should be adding to the information contained in the case through the teaching process. It offers instructors resources they could use to deepen their knowledge of the subject matter being taught.

A teaching note also gives insights as to how the case could be taught; from the questions the students should prepare before the class based on their reading of the case, to the showcasing of a plan for the case teaching session. The teaching note includes possible answers to the assignment questions that are there at the end of a case and may include a range of additional materials that could be used by the professors. A teaching note has often proved to be of immense importance to those instructors who are new to teaching cases as they get to understand the nuances of case teaching methodology. The teaching note is a document which is not shown to the organization or person about whom the case has been written.

Since a teaching note is an output based on high-end technical research activity and which is something that can make or break a case as far as its salability and usability is concerned, it needs to be effectively structured for maximizing its utility among the target audiences. *The Case Centre* (previously known as The European Case Clearing House or ECCH) has suggested a structure for compiling teaching notes on its website that has been highlighted in (**Exhibit-I**).

Exhibit-I: Components of a Teaching Note

1. **Synopsis of the case**
   Provide a brief description of what the case is about, and the context in which it is set.
2. **Target group**
   Indicate the target learning group, for example, undergraduates, postgraduates, executive.
3. **Learning objectives and key issues**
   Set out the learning objectives, and identify the key issues in the case that will help achieve them.
4. **Teaching strategy**
   Describe how the case may be used in class. For example, suggest trigger questions to open the case discussion; offer ideas for group work; suggest how learning can be consolidated at the end of the case session, and so on. This section will generally reflect your own teaching style.
5. **Questions for discussion**
   Include a list of questions designed to promote discussion of the key issues within the case.
6. **Analysis of data**
   If the case contains quantitative data for analysis it can be helpful if the results of essential 'number crunching' are provided in the teaching note. Teachers can use this to check their own calculations.
7. **Background reading**
   Provide references to relevant supplementary material on the case or related issues. You may also provide information on 'what happened next', something students are usually keen to know.
8. **Experience of using the case**
   Include feedback on how the case has worked in different classes, and the issues on which students have tended to focus. This can be useful for other teachers preparing to teach your case.
9. **Multimedia**
   Include links to video and audio clips that are relevant to the case.

Before we take a detailed look at the structure of teaching notes, let's first understand what the best practices of compiling teaching notes are; what the mistakes that teaching note developers often make are and finally how to produce a differentiated and useful teaching note for a case study.

Best Practices for Teaching Notes:

- It is often recommended to draft an outline of the teaching note before writing the case itself. The first four segments of a teaching note (viz. synopsis, issues, learning objectives and audience/prerequisites) at least need to be drafted.

- Drafting the outline of a teaching note facilitates a case author to structure the case and in data collection.
- Once this phase is over, the drafting of the case is done along with its teaching note.
- It is further recommended that the teaching note is finalized only after one or two tests, preferably with different audiences. This enables feedback from the instructor as well as from the students, about possible improvements that can be made to the case or the accompanying note.

Common Errors with Teaching Note Development:

- The teaching note and the case study often are mismatched, especially when the teaching objectives are not achievable.
- The answers to assignment questions mentioned in the teaching note are either not feasible, or too easy for the students to find.
- The teaching note is low on information that is needed for a faculty (who is not the case author) to teach the case in class.
- The teaching note offers too few alternative solutions to the case questions, which disables a professor from using the case optimally.
- Another serious mistake is not testing a case in classroom, which doesn't make for a good quality teaching note, since it would lack precious feedback about learning objectives, teaching plan, analysis, level of difficulty, etc.
- The author does away with some details considered as obvious by him but are otherwise quite significant.
- The teaching note lacks the ideal or recommended length. It is either too short (not informative enough) or too long (not concise enough).

Developing a Differentiated Teaching Note:

- The developer needs to explain all major and minor components of a teaching note vividly.
- It does add to the quality of a teaching note if the writer adds an epilogue to the note that informs about what actually happened or the decisions eventually made by the company.
- The teaching note should offer information about how the data were collected, and whether they are disguised.
- The teaching note should mention other lessons learned from the case apart from the primary learning objective.
- The teaching plan within the note should be flexible in treatment so that the teaching note can be used with different audiences. All possible teaching plans to be listed and the difficulty levels of the questions are to be clarified in the teaching note.
- Better quality control of teaching note can be ensured if the case study is tested by instructors different from the author. This can allow timely and effective improvisations to be made to the case and note.

Structuring Teaching Notes

As mentioned earlier, an effective teaching note calls for suitable structuring and over here the recommended structure has been discussed. Although variations to this structure is permissible but then teaching note and case writers should ensure that the essence or purpose of teaching note is not compromised with. The following are the components of a teaching note:

Synopsis: This being the first component, the author should give an overview of the case. Certain aspects like a company's situation and the interesting facets of the case should be mentioned. For published teaching cases, the synopsis is the part that appears in catalogues, so one must ensure that it is brief and appealing, in order to attract faculty who are in search of case studies for their courses.

Key Issues: Over here, the author should be explaining the immediate issue, which concerns what the students need to do as they are in the decision makers' shoes. The basic issue that needs mention is the concept emphasized in the case and something that motivated an instructor to choose and use the case.

Learning Outcomes/Objectives: This should contain a list of what the student should be able to learn after having discussed the case. The component needs to be as detailed and precise as possible. The number of objectives may vary according to the scope of the issue. It makes sense for the author to explain why the objectives are relevant, and consistent with the teaching plan.

Target Audiences & Prerequisites: The author is supposed to explain the audience for the case study over here (undergraduate/graduate students, MBA students, Executive MBA students, etc.). This part also mentions the prerequisites that should be understood and imbibed by the students prior to discussing the case.

Teaching Plan: This is an extremely crucial component as it is over here that the case author explains the potential roadmap for classroom discussion of a case study. Explanations are given mainly about the teaching phases, the work teams, the assignments (presentations, role-plays...), the timetable of the session as a whole and the detailed timing for each phase. The teaching plan clarifies the questions in the case study, and gives a brief description of the case discussion, which is clearly linked to reinforcing the learning objectives. A sample teaching plan could look something like as it is show in (**Exhibit-II**).

Exhibit-II: Sample Teaching Plan

- *15 minutes:* Introduction - get the class to vote on a key question e.g. Is this company financially stable? Then elicit from the class the reasons given by those who voted yes and those who voted no.

- *5 minutes:* The instructor could show a YouTube clip referenced under additional materials illustrating the context of the study.

- *25 minutes:* Assignment question 1 – the instructor shows the relevant academic model from the teaching note exhibit and gets the class to discuss how the details of the case correspond to the model.

- *35 minutes:* Assignment question 2 – the instructor gets the class to work in pairs to come up with a suggested action plan for the protagonist/company – the instructor randomly selects two pairs of students to present their plans – and then presents a framework given in the teaching note exhibit to assist the students in making decisions in the future.

- *5 minutes:* Conclusion restating the key learning points or reading the postscript.

Source: https://gbsn.org/writing-teaching-note-make-less-frightening/

Placement of the Case: This component is about the author suggesting possibilities of placing the case in a particular course, according to the learning objectives, the prerequisites, the audience and the case type. A case based on multiple issues and theoretical concepts can be used across subject domains in a course or in different related courses.

Case Analysis: In this crucial part of the teaching note, the author maps out all possible answers to the assignments questions given at the end of the case study, sorts them according to their relevance, and indicates which of the answers would be most appropriate one. Issues raised in a case study can have multiple solutions and hence it is recommended to explain the diversity of points of view and approaches, with the pros and cons of each alternative.

Teaching Aids: Over here, the author mentions all materials that facilitate a professor to use the case like videos, presentations, websites, worksheets, advertising material, product samples, annual reports etc.

Teaching Experiences/Feedback: Some teaching notes have this component where the experiences of using a case study in a class are shared. This part is written after the first classroom test is conducted with an aim to verify the following:

- The case is meeting the learning objectives mentioned
- The teaching plan is feasible
- The students are able to comprehend and deal with the case situation
- The students are able to organize, classify and combine available data
- The students understand the appropriateness of the case study
- The placement of the case in the course is relevant

Background/Additional Reading: The developer of a teaching note over here author suggests some readings for the students to be done prior to the case discussion, in order to prepare for the case effectively and bring in informed learning to class relevant to a case. This part may also include additional resources for the use of instructor. A variety of references like book chapters, journals, Internet, etc. may be suggested.

Board Plan: Any effective teaching note should have something called a board plan which is an exhibit that visually outlines the structure, sections and content of the classroom discussion, as captured by the instructor on a board in the room. Presentation of board plan within a teaching note may be graphical or textual but essentially it's a suggestion to a faculty as how to execute the case discussion in class.

TEACHING NOTE TO CASE FLYER

Celebrity Endorsements and Brands: Made for Each Other?

Synopsis

The case flyer discusses the backlash that online retailer Snapdeal had to go through in social media after its brand ambassador Aamir Khan made certain comments in the media regarding the government policy in his personal capacity. The articles based on which the case flyer has been developed presents conflicting viewpoints regarding the flipside of adopting celebrity endorsements as a tool to promote brands. The case flyer offers ample space to debate the pros and cons of celebrity endorsements and it further highlights the fact that celebrity endorsements in India need to be backed by greater wisdom of marketers as far as selecting and signing celebrities for endorsements is concerned.

Expected Learning Outcomes

- Debating the need for celebrity endorsements to be adopted by marketers/advertisers
- Analyzing the dual effect of celebrities on brands
- Brainstorming ways of enhancing effectiveness of celebrity endorsements

Placement of the Case

The case flyer can be used in the following courses:

a) Advertising and Promotion
b) Brand Management
c) Business Strategy

Suggested Route Map

Prior to discussing the Case Flyer in Classroom

a) Students were asked to read the article Celebrity Endorsement in India – *Celebrity Endorsement-A Literature Review*[1]. Reading this article would give them considerable and practical idea regarding celebrity endorsements as a brand promotion tool.

b) Students were advised to analyze all the assignment questions given at the end of case flyer (either individually or in groups) to enable them to make effective contributions in the case discussion.

During the Case Flyer discussion in Classroom

The Case flyer can be discussed effectively under three broad heads as detailed in the next page:

I Celebrity Endorsements: To be or Not To Be	II Celebrity Endorsement: A Double-edged Sword	III Celebrity Endorsements: Ways of Enhancing their Effectiveness	Wrapping Up/Debriefing
A Celebrity vs. Non-celebrity advertising B Celebrity endorsements across product categories **Discussion Facets** 1 The basic premise of success for celebrity and non-celebrity advertising is same viz. advertisement plot and its 'fit' with the brand's target group 2 Celebrity endorsements have certain obvious advantages like instant awareness and recall but then to what extent do they translate into actual sale of products. Further to what extent is the positive 'rub-off' effect of endorsements happening on brands across product categories. 3. A discussion on how can marketers modify endorsement contracts with celebrities in this age of active social media usage by customers to nullify its 'troll' effects that can be triggered as a response to some controversial celebrity action	A The pros and cons of celebrity endorsements and their corresponding effects B Customer reactions to controversial celebrity actions **Discussion Facets** 1 Celebrity endorsements have both positive and negative effects but then marketers need to analyze which of these effects are more long term in nature 2 Discussing the negative effects on brands due to their endorser actions 3 Debating the wisdom of consumer actions to Aamir Khan's personal opinion regarding government policy in the media	A The process of signing celebrities for brands B Revamping celebrity endorsement contracts **Discussion Facets** 1 The thought of bringing celebrities on board for brand promotions has been superficial on the part of marketers. The need for suitable endorsement plot, suitable celebrity-brand fit and celebrity-target audience match to be discussed 2 Brainstorming on to what extent celebrities are to have their personal space in public domain when they are endorsers of brands 3 Analyzing ways to make endorsement contracts more viable and insulated from unforeseen troubles for brands and their owners	Reiterating the learning from the case discussion and arriving at the 'big picture' emerging from the discussion
Suggested Duration: 15 minutes	Suggested Duration: 20 minutes	Suggested Duration: 20 minutes	Suggested Duration: 5 minutes

Prepared by the Author

The flow of questions during classroom discussion have been mentioned in the Board Plan [**Annexure (TN)-I**].

I Celebrity Endorsements: To Be or Not To Be

- The class was initiated by asking the students to recall few contemporary advertisements featuring celebrities for better involvement in the topic for further discussion on the subject. Also their general

understanding of celebrity endorsements was solicited by the faculty.
- Next the class discussed on the basic factors that enable endorsements to click for brands and over here the class debated on whether a celebrity or the advertisement plot/content plays a bigger role in effective brand promotion
- The class then analyzed the extent to which celebrity endorsements as a brand promotion technique is effetive across product categories. Points to dicsuss over here was if any difference in effectiveness exists between low and high involvement purchases and between goods and services as product categories.
- The class then debated that in this era of active social media participation by people (who are incidentally customers of various brands) do celebrity endorsements pose greater risk for brands or not.

II Celebrity Endorsement: A Double-edged Sword

- After learning the pros and cons of celebrity endorsements in the previous section, the class in this section debated whether it were the postive effects or the negative effects of celebrity endorsements that were more long term in nature. While many believed that controversies surrounding a celebrity was a short term affair since public memory regarding such events were short term in nature but then some felt otherwise.
- The class then analyzed and presented their view points on whether brands should at all be affected by the personal opinions that celebrities make in public domain. Celebrities are supposed to have a

private space and can an opinion that least concerns a brand in question actually hamper the prospects of a brand?
- The class then went on to discuss and debate consumer reaction in social media to Aamir Khan's personal views regarding government policy in the media. The class discussed to what extent the social media users were justified in their actions.

III Celebrity Endorsements: Ways of Enhancing their Effectivenss

- In this section, the class discussed the necessity for marketers to not just look at short term gains by signing a celebrity who will garner customer eyeballs for the brand but also the necessity to leverage a celebrity's image to a brand's advantage. The class discussed ways and means of achieving the above said objective.
- Next, the class debated as whether companies should impose restrictions on celebrities regarding what they can say or do in their personal capacity while they are in contract with a company as their brand endorser.
- Finally the class discussed regarding how to make endorsement contracts more effective and 'watertight' so that celebrities are more conscious of their responsibilities towards brands. Endorsement contracts need to be categorical about things stated so that there is little scope of misunderstanding between the parties and it works equally in favour of celebrities and brands they are endorsing for.

Wrapping Up/Debriefing

The last 5 minutes of the session were used to debrief the class based on major aspects dicussed in the previous 55 minutes of the session.

The debriefing session was about reiterating the major aspects regarding endorsements, pros and cons attached with it and how it needs a revamp to be in tune with changing times and active social media usage.

Decoding the Big Picture

Celebrity endorsements obviously has its advanatges but then marketers should be prudent enough to execute it as a promotional tool across product categories and they also need to revamp endorsement contracts to nullify any negative impact on brands due to celebrities.

Background Readings

- Agrawal, Pradeep and Dubey, S.K. (2012), "Celebrities: The Linking Pin between Brands & Their Customer", *International Journal of Management & Business Studies*, 2(1), 56-60

- Erdogan, Zafer B (1999), "Celebrity Endorsement: A Literature Review", *Journal of Marketing Management*, 15, 291-314

- Patra, Supriyo and Datta, Saroj K. (2010), "Celebrity Endorsement in India- Emerging Trends and Challenges", 5(3), 16-23

- Sonwalkar, Jayant, Kapse, Manohar and Pathak, Anuradha (2011), "Celebrity Impact – A Model of Celebrity Endorsement", *Journal of Marketing & Communication*, 7(1), 34-40

Annexure (TN) – I: Board Plan

Celebrity Endorsements: To Be or Not To Be	Celebrity Endorsement: A Double-edged Sword	Celebrity Endorsements: Ways of Enhancing their Effectiveness
The following questions were discussed in this section:	The following questions were discussed in this section:	The following questions were discussed in this section:
1 'Celebrity endorsements are no different than other form of advertising as because it is driven by an idea and if the idea works well with the target audience, the endorsements will work too else it is doomed to fail.' Do you agree? Enumerate your thoughts. 2 'Not all product categories require a celebrity.' Present your view point on this statement. 3 Opposing the idea of	1 The negative effects of celebrity endorsements are ephemeral while its positive effects are long term in nature. Cite your observations in favor of or against this statement. 2 "This is a flawed logic. Brands don't buy into brand ambassadors' personal opinions. @snapdeal shouldn't face this," Do you agree with Bansal's statement? Present your observations with suitable reasoning.	1 "With so much riding on the image of a celebrity and companies willing to devote a large chunk of their budget to ensure that a famous face brings visibility to the brand and boosts sales, most marketeers in their rush to sign up a celebrity, fail to tap into the different ways in which a celebrity's persona could colour the brand." How do you propose to amend this flawed approach

celebrity endorsements, Suhel Seth opined, "Brands carry a huge risk when they do so. Celebrity pre-hire contracts and processes aren't watertight in our country and the clauses are limited to money, appearances and conflicting categories. With social media on troll mode, celebrities often lead themselves to being exposed and result in a discussion, unnecessary for the brand." Make a critical appreciation of Seth's statement.	3 '..thousands of users deleted its app and threatened to disassociate themselves from the brand that Aamir Khan endorses.' As a consumer of brands around you, do you subscribe to such consumer actions? Present your thoughts in detail.	of marketers?

2 Should restrictions be imposed on celebrities in the celebrity contract as far as saying or doing things in one's 'personal capacity' is concerned? Present your view point through appropriate reasoning.

3 Suggest certain aspects to be incorporated in the pre-hire contracts signed with celebrities to make such documents more 'watertight'? |
| *Prepared by the Author* | | |

TEACHING NOTE TO CASE STUDY

Xiaomi in India: The Rise of the Chinese Challenger in Indian Smartphone Market

Synopsis

The case study details the rise of Xiaomi in the Indian smartphone market. There were certain distinct lacunae existing in the Indian smartphone market that Xiaomi addressed right at the start of its operations in India in 2014. The company successfully tackled the initial operational hurdles and wooed the Indian customers with smartphones that well defined the idea of value proposition. Sustained constructive efforts in the Indian markets along with building a loyal consumer community around the brand allowed Xiaomi to surpass Samsung as the leader in the smartphone category in India.

Prerequisite Conceptual Understanding

The participants/students of the case discussion should have a working knowledge along with the business implications of the following concepts viz. Segmentation-Targeting-Positioning, Market entry strategies, Marketing Mix and Distribution. Suitable case discussion will be facilitated if the students read the above mentioned concepts in the book titled *Marketing Management*, 14th Edition, Prentice Hall, 2011 by Philip Kotler.

Expected Learning Outcomes

- To analyze and comprehend the marketing strategies adopted by Xiaomi to enter Indian smartphone market

- To examine the initial failures/stumbling blocks faced by Xiaomi in India

- To analyze the factors that have contributed to the success of Xiaomi in Indian smartphone market

Placement of the Case

The case study can be used to develop a practical understanding of the following topics in Marketing Management:

a) Segmentation-Targeting-Positioning
b) Marketing Mix
c) Market entry Strategies
d) Distribution Strategies

Assignment Question

1. What are the various marketing strategies to be used by an international marketer in its global expansion efforts?

2. Comment on the market entry strategies adopted by Xiaomi for the Indian market?

3. What were the major stumbling blocks that Xiaomi initially experienced in India?

4. How did Xiaomi go about addressing the 'availability quotient' of its smartphones in India?

5. What have been the various factors that have contributed to Xiaomi's success in India?

6. What are the aspects that have worked in favor of Xiaomi and the potential challenges it faces in India?

Case Analysis

The classroom discussion could be summarized through the Board Plan [**Exhibit (TN)-I**]. The Board Plan presents a graphical representation of the flow of discussing the case study in class. The classroom discussion was executed under three broad categories as explained below.

Topic of Discussion	Marketing Strategies of Xiaomi in India	Problem Areas of Xiaomi	Improvisation & Sustainable Growth
Central Point of Discussion	Market entry by an international marketer in a saturated foreign market	The initial stumbling blocks faced by Xiaomi in India	Improvisations made by Xiaomi and the subsequent and sustainable growth
Highlights of Discussion	*Market entry strategies adopted by Xiaomi for Indian market *The marketing strategies that caused a disruption in Indian market	*The various issues/hurdles faced by Xiaomi initially in India	*The improvisations made by Xiaomi to its marketing mix *The various other factors contributing to its sustainable growth
Duration	15 minutes	20 minutes	20 minutes

Prepared by the Author

Case Analysis and Class Discussion

*Marketing Strategies of Xiaomi in India

What are the various marketing strategies that a global marketer can adopt in its expansion efforts?

Ansoff's matrix can be used over here to unravel four viable strategies open to a global marketer. Quadrant 1 of the matrix involves delivering existing products to existing customers. Quadrant 2 involves offering new products to existing customers. Quadrant 3 involves finding new customers for existing products while Quadrant 4 involves offering new products to new customers which in other words is about diversification being adopted by a company.

	Products	
Markets	Exisiting	New
Exisiting	Market Penetration	Product Development
New	Market Development	Diversification

Source: https://thecimastudent.com/2016/11/16/cima-e2-ansoffs-matrix/

What do you understand by the term market entry strategy?

A market entry strategy is described as a planned method of delivering goods or services to a new target market and distributing them there. Companies need to think about various issues as they make a decision to enter new markets. The options vary with cost, risk and degree of control. Simple entry strategies involve direct (agent) or indirect (counter trade) method while complex forms involve joint ventures or export processing zones. The market entry framework has been shown below:

Market assessment	• Legal and regulatory assessment • Market & competition assessment	• Customer assessment • Internal strength & weakness assessment
Business case development	• Market attractiveness • Partner selection & analysis	• Entry barrier assessment • Financial analysis (cash flow)
Implementation strategy	• Partnership negotiation & structure • Entry plan blueprint	• Strategic planning
G'LIVE!	• Management of organization • Governance • Recruitment & training	• Change management • Business development

Source: http://www.business-fundas.com/2010/market-entry-strategy/

Comment on the market entry strategy of Xiaomi in India?

Xiaomi adopted go-to-market strategy of selling its smartphones only via e-commerce. Xiaomi signed an exclusive contract with Flipkart and executed 'flash sales' for its new model launches. 'Flash sales' is a marketing technique that creates an artificial sense of urgency/crisis in buyers to buy the devices the very moment they are available. Xiaomi's 'flash sale' is a well thought-through company strategy that focuses of keeping the bottom-line of the company growing. Value based pricing (offering compatible devices with aggressive pricing strategy) was definitely another highlight of Xiaomi's market entry in India.

*Problem Areas of Xiaomi

What were the major stumbling blocks that Xiaomi initially faced in India?

Despite doing incredibly well in the first ever 'flash sales' in India, the first significant hurdle was the irrational large scale public disdain for Chinese products in the country and thus hailing from China was one of the negatives associated with Xiaomi. Further sloppy after sales service, non-availability of spare parts led to bitter customer experience. Resorting to denial marketing or in other words creating scenarios of artificial crisis was not quite to the liking of many. Limited distribution or low product availability were some of the other major stumbling blocks apart from heating issues with the devices, data theft allegations and patent infringement issues.

Exhibit (TN)-I: Board Plan

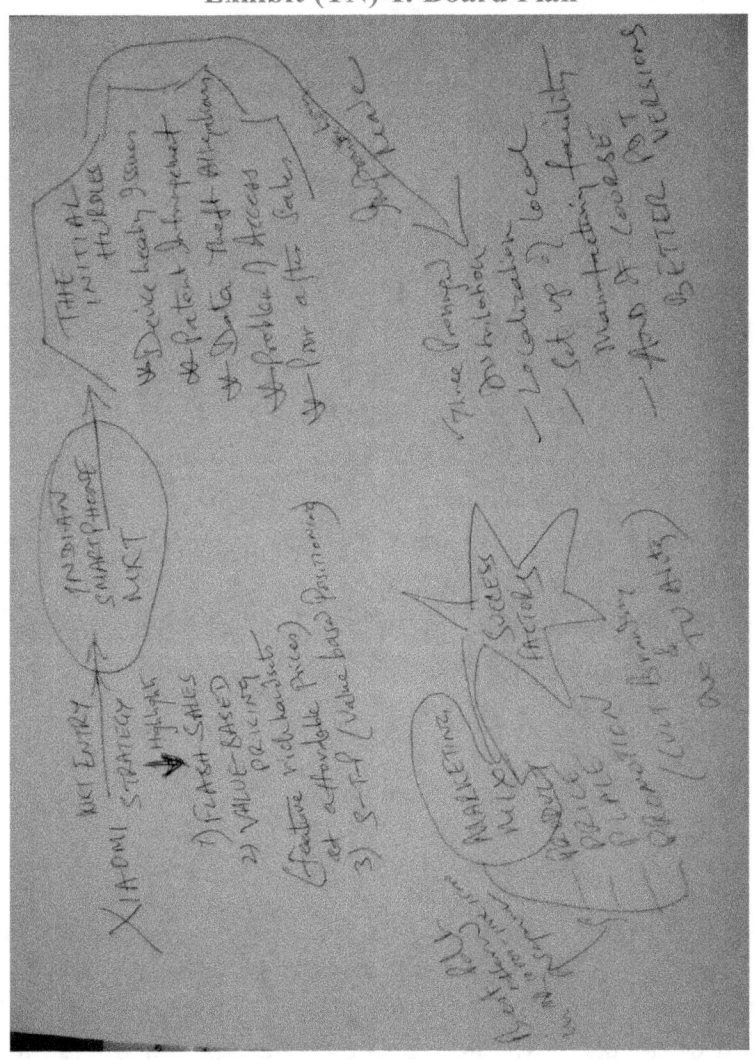

*Improvisation & Sustainable Growth

How did Xiaomi go about addressing the 'availability quotient' of its smartphones in India?

↓

Xiaomi has been consciously building capacities around online retail since 2014 and this route accounts for 30% of total smartphone sales in the country. To counter the issue of availability, Xiaomi built its offline business aggressively with a three-pronged strategy involving large format retailers, Mi Preferred Partner Stores and Mi Home Stores. Xiaomi streamlined its supply chain to make sure that the demand versus supply gap was not significant. The company set up two manufacturing facilities in the state of Andhra Pradesh where 75% of the handsets being sold in India are manufactured and this has further addressed the issue of 'availability' in India.

What have been the various factors that have contributed to Xiaomi's success in India?

↓

The marketing mix adopted by Xiaomi is analyzed. Handsets with high-end features at aggressive prices have been one of the prime success factors. An example to be cited over here in the above said context is that of Redmi Note 4. It has Qualcomm Snapdragon 625 processor, with 4GB RAM, 64GB internal storage, metal body and up to 2 days of battery life. It costs ₹13000 while any comparable brand with the above mentioned features costs anywhere between ₹18000- ₹25000. The three-pronged distribution strategy with the objective of enhancing visibility and access is another important contributor to Xiaomi's success in India. Instead of spending astronomical amounts on advertising, Xiaomi focused on building a customer community/cult around the brand. The Mi Community is the official forum for Xiaomi to interact with its customers. It has gone on to incorporate several innovative features in its handsets based on customer feedback received through this forum. One such example is the dual-SIM smartphone Redmi Y1 with a micro SD card. A look at the exhibit below shows how well Xiaomi has established its hold in the Indian smartphone market:

The top five smartphone models in India in Q3 2017

1. Xiaomi Redmi Note 4

2. Xiaomi Redmi 4

3. Xiaomi Redmi 4A

4. Samsung Galaxy J2

5. Oppo A37

Source: https://qz.com/india/1115071/samsung-beware-how-xiaomi-is-winning-over-indias-booming-smartphone-market/ ↓

What are the aspects that have worked in favor of Xiaomi and the potential challenges it faces in India?

↓

The following aspects that have worked in favor of Xiaomi in India are cited:

- Reducing marketing costs by dominating the e-retailing channels to sell handsets and doing away with traditional advertising
- Positioning Mi phones as value for money devices and not cheap devices.
- Developing a dedicated Mi Fan Community to build a cult like aura around the brand
- Maintaining strong focus on the highest growth smartphone price segment viz. ₹10000 - ₹ 15000

Some of the potential challenges for Xiaomi that are cited:

- Aggressive expansion offline may tend to stretch its resources as various fixed and variable costs will be added
- Xiaomi continues to struggle in the mid-range (₹15000 - ₹20000) segment where competitors like Samsung, Oppo and Vivo are strong
- Xiaomi lacks a diverse portfolio across varied price points to target new users
- Enhancing the number of service centers is another area of challenge

Wrapping Up/Debriefing

The last five minutes of the case discussion can be used to summarize the major takeaways from the discussion. Xiaomi executed the technique of 'flash sales' along with value-based positioning of its handsets to perfection for gaining the initial hold on the Indian smartphone market. Subsequently, although it encountered a variety of hiccups, Xiaomi learnt fast and amended the loopholes in its strategy timely which enabled it reach the pinnacle of the Indian smartphone market within four years of initiating its operations.

Decoding the Big Picture

Offering feature-rich handsets at competitive prices along with maintaining a strong focus on customer wants has propelled Xiaomi to claim the top spot in the Indian smartphone market.

Background Readings

- https://www.simpletense.com/samples/Marketing_Essay.pdf
- U N, Sushma, "How Xiaomi is winning over India's booming smartphone market", https://qz.com/india/1115071/samsung-beware-how-xiaomi-is-winning-over-indias-booming-smartphone-market/, November 2nd 2017
- Baxi, Abhishek, "The Rise and Rise of China's Xiaomi in India", https://www.forbes.com/sites/baxiabhishek/2017/09/12/the-rise-and-rise-of-chinas-xiaomi-in-india/#452c5a256789, September 12th 2017
- Singh, Rajiv, "How China's handset maker Xiaomi came first in India", https://economictimes.indiatimes.com/tech/hardware/how-chinas-handset-maker-xiaomi-came-first-in-india/articleshow/61798368.cms, November 26th 2017

PART B:

TEACHING CASE STUDIES EFFECTIVELY

Preamble to PART B

Both as a learner as well as an instructor, one needs to understand what exactly a case study is. It is not an article that is largely subjective and judgmental in nature. Unlike an author of an article, an author of a case study is supposed to be dispassionate and objective in writing a case study. He should be aware of the purpose of writing a case, the target audience for whom the case is being written, the likely course where it is to be used as a teaching tool etc.

A case study is a dispassionate and objective commentary about a company, brand, individual etc. Case studies describe real life business and management situations, issues and dilemmas and the major objective of a case is to trigger discussions and debates on the issues mentioned so that application based learning happens for the participants. There are various entities who write cases viz. case writers, research associates, educators (often educators assisted by research associates) and also by students.

Case studies can be classified based on their length, source of writing the case (based on field or secondary research), target audience (students, working executives etc.). Theoretical knowledge especially in professional courses like MBA is absolutely incomplete until and unless it is supplemented with application based education and this requires certain potent tools. Case studies or case teaching method is definitely one of them where students are motivated to think laterally, put themselves in the shoes of the decision maker and come up with effective solutions to the problems or issues raised in the case study. It also helps develop the skill of working in groups or teams which is so very much required in corporate life.

The case method of teaching aims at imparting certain skills to pupils that have been mentioned below:
- Analysis & critical thinking
- Presenting one's thoughts with clarity
- Defending and challenging viewpoints
- Working in team as well as solo
- Listening
- Cautious in decision making
- Linking theory to practice

As one can see, each and every skill mentioned above is absolutely critical in the making of a good corporate personality. These are skills that groom individuals to become industry ready for the ever challenging Indian and global markets.

The activity of teaching case studies leads to learning through case studies and there are certain beliefs associated about learning which are so true:
- People learn only when they are interested to learn
- The process of learning depends on wanting to learn
- Learning happens best when participants have the liberty to create their own responses to a situation
- Actual learning happens when participants are not knowing the answers
- Learning is an experience which is largely emotional

To further understand the concept of learning, it makes sense to take a look at the Learning Cycle proposed by David Kolb in 1984 (**Exhibit-I**). Kolb's experiential learning theory works at two levels viz. four stage of learning and four separate learning styles. As per Kolb, learning involves acquiring abstract concepts that can be applied flexibly to a range of situations. An instructor thus need to cease being a teacher and rather be a facilitator while initiating and conducting case discussions and this will ensure flexibility in the learning process. As per the learning cycle proposed by Kolb, a learner touches all the 'bases'.

Exhibit-I: Kolb's Learning Cycle

Concrete Experience
(doing / having an experience)

Active Experimentation
(planning / trying out what you have learned)

Reflective Observation
(reviewing / reflecting on the experience)

Abstract Conceptualisation
(concluding / learning from the experience)

Source: https://www.simplypsychology.org/learning-kolb.html

Effective learning through case based teaching methodology can only happen when a person progresses through a cycle of four stages viz. having a concrete experience followed by observation and reflection on that experience that leads to formation of abstract concepts and conclusions which are then used to test hypothesis in future situations, resulting in new experiences.

In this second part of the book that is about teaching case studies effectively, I have taken the Xiaomi case study once again to ensure consistency throughout this book. In this part, I will demonstrate how to teach this case study effectively in class or in other words how can students learn effectively through this case study about the concepts etc. discussed in it. There is a certain way to approach case learning and that is what is going to be stated in this part. As a teacher believing in and executing case based education, he/she needs to ensure that this approach is adhered to by students in order to have purposeful, active and application based learning.

THE SAMPLE CASE STUDY

Please note that while going through a case study in detail, it needs to be annotated at places that you as a reader feel will be important in case analysis. Important personalities mentioned in the case or events and their contribution to the case timeline needs annotation for later reference. Annotations can include highlights, underlines or comments at appropriate places within the case.

Xiaomi in India: The Rise of the Chinese Challenger in Indian Smartphone Market

"I believe our constant innovation across our products, operating model and our commitment to India has helped us win over our MI fans."

- Manu Jain (Vice President, Xiaomi India)

Indian smartphone market has always been a play field of Nokia, Apple and Samsung where smartphones meant a premium to pay. Manufacturers like Micromax, Lava etc. were making phones but they never gave that ease and freedom to the consumers. Xiaomi entered India in 2014. The first phone MI3 was a mid-range phone but then a significant event happened when Xiaomi started selling budget series phone Redmi 1s. The manufacturer created a niche for its smartphone brand by executing flash sales on online shopping sites like Flipkart, which resulted in stock outs within matter of minutes. Hugo Barra former VP of Xiaomi India was more focused on the budget range as he felt that the Indian smartphone market was a price sensitive market. It was really incredible to find the brand rising to the top of the charts toppling its established competitors like Samsung without any celebrity endorsements or intensive marketing efforts. Value based pricing was one of the major reasons for the success of Xiaomi in India. This strategy helped build a community around the brand. Innovative and high performance phones and accessories have enabled Xiaomi develop an interesting and saleable product portfolio over the years.

A Humble Beginning
2014 was the year when Xiaomi India held an event to launch their first phone MI3 in India, Hugo Barra launched the phone at a staggering and ground breaking price of ₹13,999 when the phones with same specifications were no way near the price

Exhibit - I: Price Comparison of MI3 and LG Nexus 5

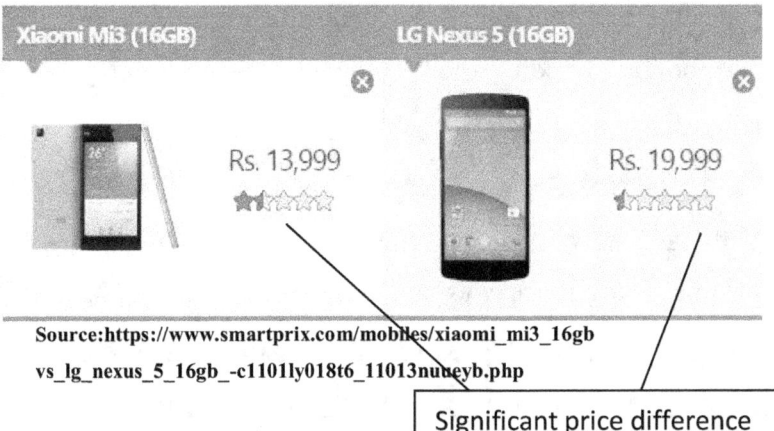

Source:https://www.smartprix.com/mobiles/xiaomi_mi3_16gb vs_lg_nexus_5_16gb_-c1101ly018t6_11013nuueyb.php

Significant price difference

Xiaomi has always been the company that has priced their products closest to their bill of material without compromising the component quality and performance compared to other premium smartphones. That has been the key to their success. Xiaomi cashed on people's new found interest in buying electronic gadgets online and thus they effectively placed their first product on Flipkart. After the success of Redmi 1s the company looked to go for the release of different and advanced models of smartphone from its stable like MI3 and MI4. The phone did not hit the Indian shores like the previous ones. Then the company came with more pocket friendly Redmi 2 which was also value for money device. Xiaomi soon started getting better vibes from the market.

Hurdles on the way

Even after becoming the new cynosure of the Indian smartphone market the company faced many challenges. Complaints of heating issues were on the rise as the Mi4 hit the market. Sales were tumbling down even after being a mid-range device as the consumer experience was not quite satisfactory. The most controversial device of Xiaomi India was the Redmi Note 3G as people were accusing the company for data theft and sending the data to the Chinese servers (**Exhibit-II**).

Not only this but the Redmi Note 3G was also found to get into turmoil because of patent infringement with

Ericson. Another challenge was in the area of establishing greater number of service centers as the existing number was not quite wholesome from customer service viewpoint plus competitors like ASUS were also making their presence felt in the increasingly saturated Indian smartphone market.

Exhibit-II: Gaqdgets360 reports Data Theft

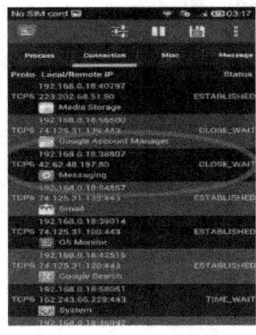

OCWorkbench, citing a Taiwanese publication, suggested that the budget Xiaomi Redmi Note, which was announced for the Indian market alongside the Mi 3 (Review | Pictures), was secretly sending data to a China-based server.

In addition, [the OCWorkbench report notes] a Hong Kong-based IMA Mobile user Kenny Li claims to have tested the Redmi Note smartphone, and found it was automatically connecting to an IP address hosted in China and sending data back when connected to a Wi-Fi network. Li also claimed that the Xiaomi Redmi Note was sending information to the Chinese server at a much lower data transmission rate when connected to a 3G network.

Interestingly, the Redmi Note was reportedly found transmitting data in the background even after being rooted or after being flashed with another firmware on top. OCWorkbench speculates that the transmission process had been hardcoded into the Xiaomi Redmi Note. The site noted that the company's cloud service called MiCloud was switched off during the testing.

Source: https://gadgets.ndtv.com/mobiles/news/is-xiaomi-secretly-sending-smartphone-user-data-to-chinese-servers-567686

Serious allegations regarding data theft

Complaints regarding poor after sales service and the company's inability to meet the rising demand of consumers for Xiaomi smartphones were some of the other major issues The later contributed to reports of black marketing of Miphones.

Journey to the top

As on date, the company has been there in Indian market for quite sometime. The company has been expanding its dealer network across the country and is also in the process of launching new exclusive stores to showcase its range of products.

Xiaomi has been selling its smartphones both in the online as well as in the offline space and it has been observed that the major part of the smartphone buying is happening in the offline space. The company has been targeting the selfie obsessed audiences in both online and offline channels with its select products. Xiaomi not only tied up with stores where they can sell products offline but also they set-up MI HOME (exclusive Xiaomi outlets across India), similar to the execution of Apple stores where people can experience the products and buy them. The sale reports reflected the growth in the market share of the company after the nationwide set-up of the MI HOMEs. In 2018, the company ranks 2nd in terms of market share in the Indian smartphone market (**Exhibit-III**).

Exhibit-III: The IDC quarterly report of Q2 in 2017

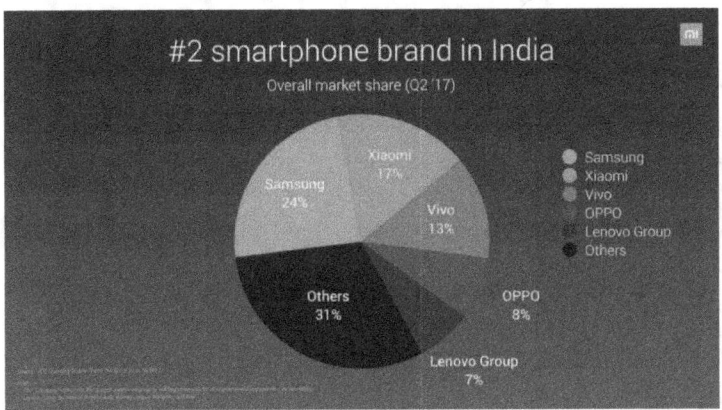

Xiaomi was forecasted to surpass Samsung after the year 2017 but the company managed to achieve that feat by the end of Q4 of 2017; the credit for which should go to the success of Redmi Note 4 as it was the most sold smartphone of the year 2017 (**Exhibit-IV**).

Credit not only goes to the product but also to the community the company has been building around its products. MI Forums, MI Community have significant role to play in the success of the company. The community members known as MI Fans have always been given sufficient regard and recognition by Xiaomi which has made consumer bonding with the company stronger over time.

Exhibit-IV: The IDC quarterly report Q4 2017

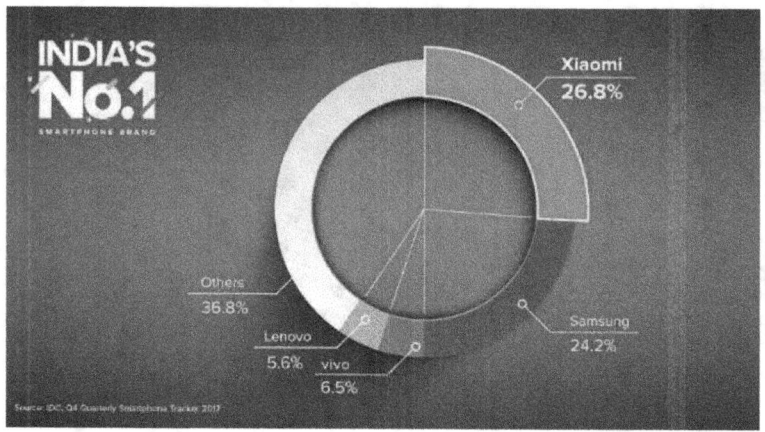

The trend of replacing smartphones on frequent basis has been on the rise mostly among the youth in this country and Xiaomi has cashed on this opportunity by launching more budget friendly quality devices. The value based pricing of Xiaomi made sure that competitors like Micromax's YU brand fail to keep the Chinese handset maker concerned for long. One of the contributors for the low pricing of Xiaomi is the 'Make in India' initiative taken by Xiaomi, opening two manufacturing facilities in India[11]. This has saved import duty and helped in developing customer-friendly pricing for their products giving them an edge over competition. Xiaomi have also treaded the path of future proofing their phones with narrowing down their displays of the phone which started with MI MIX line up. MI MIX line-up said to be the concept phone for the consumers as it reflected their futuristic design of no-edge displays.

The Road Ahead

Xiaomi, as per industry reports is the market leader in the Indian smartphone territory which leads to the question of how cans the company maintain its lead over competition? The company is presently more focused on bringing their ecosystem products like MI Band, MI TV and MI Bag pack etc. to the Indian market. MI has always focused on the innovation and bringing the products at best prices possible. The company might look to cement their place at the top but there are established competitors like Samsung, ASUS. The moves that Xiaomi make need to be differentiated and as per market requirements so that they keep striking the right chord with customers.

Assignment Questions

1. What are the various marketing strategies to be used by an international marketer in its global expansion efforts?

2. Comment on the market entry strategies adopted by Xiaomi for the Indian market?

3. What were the major stumbling blocks that Xiaomi initially experienced in India?

4. How did Xiaomi go about addressing the 'availability quotient' of its smartphones in India?

5. What have been the various factors that have contributed to Xiaomi's success in India?

6. What are the aspects that have worked in favor of Xiaomi and the potential challenges it faces in India?

THE CASE TEACHING METHODOLOGY

The first action that an instructor needs to take for making classes learn effectively through case studies is circulate a document called *Case Comprehension Checklist* along with the case study that preferably has assignment questions at the end of it. Students are required to put a tick mark against various activities mentioned in the document once they complete it and also jot down certain details of the information they extract from the case study. Readers of the book will find the Xiaomi case study in Part B of this book annotated at various places and there is a reason to it which will be mentioned later in this part of the book.

Before proceeding further with the case teaching method, let's first take a look at the most critical document accompanying a case study which will enable students to learn through a case in the most effective way and that is the *Case Comprehension Checklist* (**Exhibit-II**). The template of which is presented in the following page.

Exhibit-II: *Case Comprehension Checklist*

CASE COMPREHENSION CHECKLIST

Phase I: Know Your Case Study

RECOMMENDED SEQUENCE OF STEPS	
Go through the Opening Paragraph	☐
Go through the Final Paragraph	☐
Read the Subheads	☐
Go through the Exhibits & Annexure	☐
Go through the Assignment questions	☐
Recall the course/subject area for which this case is meant	☐
Go through the case study thoroughly	☐
Develop a timeline of the events mentioned in case study	☐

Phase II: Know the Key People & Issues

RECOMMENDED SEQUENCE OF STEPS	
Primary Character in the Case:	ENTER DETAILS
Supporting Character in the Case:	ENTER DETAILS
The Primary Issue in the Case:	ENTER DETAILS
Other Issues in the Case:	ENTER DETAILS

Continued....

Phase III: Dissect Your Case Study

RECOMMENDED SEQUENCE OF STEPS	
Theories, Models and Frameworks that will help me:	ENTER DETAILS HERE
Important/Significant Numerals mentioned in the Case:	ENTER DETAILS HERE
Any extra data that will further enable understanding the Case:	ENTER DETAILS HERE
Where is this additional data available:	ENTER DETAILS HERE
Assumptions made OR need to be made:	ENTER DETAILS HERE

Phase IV: Decide & Execute

RECOMMENDED SEQUENCE OF STEPS	
Proposed courses of action to address issues/ problems mention in case:	ENTER DETAILS HERE
Evaluating the Options:	ENTER DETAILS HERE
Your preferred course of action:	ENTER DETAILS HERE
Evidence to Support your Preferred course of action:	ENTER DETAILS HERE
Propose the way to execute your preferred course of action:	ENTER DETAILS HERE

From the Exhibit, readers can see that the checklist comprises four phases and these phases involve a series of recommended steps. The sequence mentioned in the checklist needs to be followed for optimal results and thus instructors should advise pupils to do the same. They must also insist that the case comprehension checklist should be with them while they are working on the case alone or in groups and they must carry this document for case discussion in class as this will help them track how they travelled through a case study to reach certain conclusions.

The first purpose of the checklist is to know a case study well or in other words get familiar with the case study given by the instructor. Students need to read the introductory paragraph, the final paragraph, the exhibits, tables etc, the subheads, the assignment questions and all this will make the student get an initial feel and grip of the case study. The next step in the first phase involves going thoroughly through the case study and finally making a timeline of events mentioned in the case study. As one completes each step in Phase I of the checklist, they should put a tick against the step mentioned.

The next purpose of case comprehension is to know the characters of the case study well. Knowing the CEO, Director or such other individual who is at the helm of affairs and also various supporting characters like the Regional Manager or the venture capitalist for a firm on whom a case has been developed. In the Xiaomi case study, Manu Jain, vice-president of Xiaomi India is the primary character. Hugo Barra can be referred to as the supporting character in the context of the case. The primary issue of the case study are the factors that have enabled the company to be the leader in the Indian smartphone market while the secondary issue will be the initial roadblocks faced and the potential challenges for the company. As per the template of the checklist all these details need to be entered in appropriate place. The completed checklist after the four phases has been shown in an exhibit later in this book. While going through the case study thoroughly and for the purpose of extracting crucial information and data for analysis, the instructor needs to demonstrate how to annotate a case study for easier referral at various occasions before and during case discussion.

The third phase of the case comprehension checklist is about dissecting a case study. Over here, first of all students need to make note of the theories and frameworks that will help them to comprehend the case study better. Next they should make note of those numerals mentioned in the case study that are significant. It is this phase of the case analysis where an instructor needs to suggest his pupils to identify the need for extra data that will help them to get a better grip of the case study and enjoy additional advantage during case discussion. The instructor initially also needs to facilitate students in identifying sources from where this extra can be obtained. The students over here also should be making note of the assumptions they have made to answer the assignment questions or the assumptions they need to make. Necessary inputs related to the Xiaomi case study have been provided in the filled up template of the checklist exhibited later on.

The final phase of the checklist is about taking pertinent decisions and executing them. In the checklist one needs to enter details like proposed course of action to address the issues/problems; evaluating the various options thought of and choosing the best course of action based on certain parameters and assumptions. Finally they need to jot down how the proposed course of action can be executed in a feasible manner.

It is always recommended that teachers play the role of facilitator in any case teaching methodology. In other words, a teacher's involvement in case teaching and discussion is no less than the students. In fact it will be he who will be guiding and leading a class in a direction that calls for effective learning through application. The *Case Comprehension Checklist* is a potent tool that a teacher possesses in the said context. It is something that will not allow the direction of case analysis and subsequent discussion to drift. Rather it will keep each and everyone focused on how to analyze the case study effectively and thus realize the pedagogical objectives of the case.

The filled up Case Comprehension Checklist for the Xiaomi case study can be found in (**Exhibit-III**).

Exhibit-III: Filled up Case Comprehension Checklist

CASE COMPREHENSION CHECKLIST

Phase I: Know Your Case Study

RECOMMENDED SEQUENCE OF STEPS	
Go through the Opening Paragraph	✓
Go through the Final Paragraph	✓
Read the Subheads	✓
Go through the Exhibits & Annexure	✓
Go through the Assignment questions	✓
Recall the course/subject area for which this case is meant	✓
Go through the case study thoroughly	✓
Develop a timeline of the events mentioned in case study	✓

TIMELINE OF KEY EVENTS XIAOMI INDIA (2014-2018)
- 2014: Entered India
- 2014: 'Flash sales' of Redmi 1s on Flipkart
- 2017: Redmi Note 4 is the most sold phone of the year
- 2017: Xiaomi surpasses Samsung to claim the top spot in Indian smartphone market

Continued...

Phase II: Know the Key People & Issues

RECOMMENDED SEQUENCE OF STEPS	
Primary Character in the Case:	Manu Jain
Supporting Character in the Case:	Hugo Barra
The Primary Issue in the Case:	Xiaomi surpassing Samsung and thus claiming the top spot in the the Indian smartphone market
Other Issues in the Case:	Xiaomi improvised its marketing mix especially in the area of distribution to make its phones more accessible. Offering feature rich phones at affordable prices. Developing a cult following around a brand

Phase III: Dissect Your Case Study

RECOMMENDED SEQUENCE OF STEPS	
Theories, Models and Frameworks that will help me:	Ansoff's Matrix, Market entry framework, Marketing mix
Important/Significant Numerals mentioned in the Case:	From a market share of 17% in Q2'17, Xiaomi acquired a market share of 26.8% in Q4'17
Any extra data that will further enable understanding the Case:	* Data on the overall smartphone buying scenario in India *Competitive scenario especially how are the other Chinese players doing?
Where is this additional data available:	Websites of various Indian newspapers & business magazines
Assumptions made OR need to be made:	-----------

Continued...

Phase IV: Decide & Execute

RECOMMENDED SEQUENCE OF STEPS	
Proposed courses of action to address issues/ problems mention in case:	*This is a case study where incidentally all problems mentioned in the case have been taken care of. *However distribution is still an issues and so are the number of service centers. Actions need to be taken in this area *Xiaomi needs to be alert to competitive moves *Xiaomi needs to cater to the Mid-range segment by developing appropriate products to take on established players like Samsung
Evaluating the Options:	*Option 2 needs thorough perusal *Option 4 also has to be worked for long term results
Your preferred course of action:	Increasing access in Tier 2 towns and smaller cities by increasing number of outlets and service centers
Evidence to Support your Preferred course of action:	This move has already helped the company and has been a major enabler to claim the top spot in the Indian smartphone market
Propose the way to execute your preferred course of action:	*Enter into negotiations with existing phone retailers to stock Mi phones *Opening new Mi Homes in smaller towns and cities of India along with More service centers

I hope thus that instructors have understood how to make students utilize the checklist to better comprehend case studies and make themselves prepare better for case discussions.

An instructor must be aware of certain do's and don'ts associated with learning through case studies which he needs to communicate to students at opportune moments. Some of those have been listed below:

The **Do's** in case learning:
- The prospect of expressing oneself in the public domain often adds to nervousness in a person and hence it is recommended to SPEAK EARLY
- LISTENING is extremely important to effective case discussion
- BUILD on the logical and pertinent comments made by peers during discussion
- Case discussions opens up an avenue of learning and in order to learn well one needs to keep an OPEN MIND
- PUSH YOUR IDEAS when you really have something feasible and interesting in mind
- It is always recommended to bring in OUTSIDE EXPERIENCES to class for overall and holistic learning
- Have the PATIENCE and RESPECT to listen to the thoughts of peers
- It is also recommended that one can mention about LEARNING FROM A PREVIOUS CASE DISCUSSION in the course in case it is relatable.

The **Don'ts** in case learning:
- Do not BEAT ABOUT THE BUSH or REPEAT COMMENTS already made by peers
- DIGRESS from what needs to be discussed
- Do not CONCEAL FACTS AND INFORMATION in case you are sure it will help in holistic learning of class
- Do not make a MOCKERY of or BELITTLE THOUGHTS of others being shared in class
- Do not LOSE YOUR FOCUS or get distracted while the case discussion

A teacher or an instructor needs to play multiple roles while the case discussion is on. He is not just supposed to play the role of an evaluator but also an observer and moderator. The instructor needs to keenly observe the contributions being made by each and every student to the case discussion, their overall body language, their keenness to learn through the case study and see to it that at no point of time especially during events of debate, things do not go out of control. Effectively it boils down to the instructor being an active and leading participant in the case discussion and not just a passive observer of things.

An instructor can evaluate students based on their in-class participation, case analysis writing and the quality of thoughts being contributed by a student to case discussion. The instructor should offer feedback to students regarding their performance and regarding the areas where they need to pull up their socks. This ensures transparency in the evaluation mechanism and keeps students aware of how they can improve on learning through case teaching methodology.

*

About the Author

Dr. Kisholoy Roy is a PhD in Management from IIT (Indian School of Mines), Dhanbad. He is a certified Accredited Management Teacher (AMT) who has been into teaching Management for several years now at the post graduate level. Dr Roy has authored several books on management apart from authoring various case studies, articles and research papers. He is presently engaged as an independent trainer and consultant in digital marketing and brand communication apart from his engagements as a faculty in Marketing with various B-schools.

www.ingramcontent.com/pod-product-compliance
Lightning Source LLC
Chambersburg PA
CBHW071417220526
45469CB00004B/1311